Bible Knock Knocks
and Other Fun Stuff

BIBLE KNOCK KNOCKS

AND OTHER FUN STUFF

Mary Lou Carney

Illustrated by Charlie Cox

Abingdon Press / Nashville

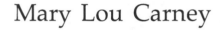

BIBLE KNOCK KNOCKS AND OTHER FUN STUFF

Text Copyright © 1988 by Mary Lou Carney
Illustrations Copyright © 1988 by Abingdon Press

Library of Congress Cataloging-in-Publication Data

Carney, Mary Lou, 1949–
   Bible knock knocks and other fun stuff.
   Summary: Presents a collection of jokes, riddles,
puns, and limericks focusing on biblical characters
and events.
   1. Bible—Juvenile humor. 2. Wit and humor,
Juvenile. 3. Limericks, Juvenile. 4. Knock-knock
jokes. [1. Bible—Wit and humor. 2. Jokes. 3. Riddles]
I. Title.
PN6231.B45C37   1988   818'.5402   88-939
ISBN 0-687-03180-X

This book is printed on recycled acid-free paper.

94 95 96 97 98 99 00 01 02—10 9 8 7 6

MANUFACTURED IN THE UNITED STATES OF AMERICA

to
my fifth-grade teacher,
who christened my first poem
with a
D

CONTENTS

INTRODUCTION

Don't you hate it when everybody talks about the joy of the Lord—but nobody smiles?

Me, too!

We Christians are the happiest people around, right? So let's let our faces show it! Smile!

Come on. You can do better than that.

Maybe what you need is a little practice, a few reasons to smile.

So here they are. One hundred and forty-five (count 'em, 145!) jokes and riddles and puns and other fun stuff. All about Noah (do you know when he loaded the ducks?) and the plagues God sent on Egypt (toadily awesome!) and Queen Esther (who had to become a protester) and Jonah (who *was* "the catch of the day") and . . .

Well, you get the idea.

So, come on, you Christians. Enjoy! Smile! Laugh!

Nobody has a better reason.

Mary Lou Carney

SOMEBODY'S KNOCKIN'

Knock, knock.
Who's there?
Jonah.
Jonah who?
Jonah church of your choice!

Knock, knock.
Who's there?
Eve.
Eve who?
Eve you've a problem, talk to God about it!

Knock, knock.
Who's there?
Phillip.
Phillip who?
Phillip with God's Holy Spirit!

Knock, knock.
Who's there?
Ruth.
Ruth who?
Ruth-er be on God's side!

Knock, knock.
Who's there?
Paul.
Paul who?
Paul yourself together and do what's right!

Knock, knock.
Who's there?
Andrew.
Andrew who?
Andrew better live for the Lord!

Knock, knock.
Who's there?
Cain.
Cain who?
Cain you be kind to others?

Knock, knock.
Who's there?
Able.
Able who?
Able to do anything—with God's help!

Knock, knock.
Who's there?
Ham.
Ham who?
Ham-per the devil whenever you can!

Knock, knock.
Who's there?
Lot.
Lot who?
Lot of great promises in the Bible!

Knock, knock.
Who's there?
Esau.
Esau who?
Esau-ful important to do what's right!

Knock, knock.
Who's there?
John.
John who?
John me in working for the Lord!

Knock, knock.
Who's there?
Luke.
Luke who?
Luke to Jesus, your best friend!

Knock, knock.
Who's there?
Acts.
Acts who?
Acts me if I love the Lord!

Knock, knock.
Who's there?
Nathan.
Nathan who?
Nathan is impossible for those who have faith!

Noah worked both long and hard
  to get the animals on.
He loaded chicks and geese by night
  and ducks at the quack of dawn.

The elephants were the first to come.
  Not a single one held back.
They were eager to be on their way.
  They had their trunks all packed.

Lions and tigers marched aboard
  to the tune of a jaybird's song.
The dromedaries boarded last—
  they were glad to camel-long!

(Genesis 7:1-5)

Noah's dear grandfather
  had a life both long and fine.
He walked with God and lived to be
  nine hundred sixty-nine!

Name him.

(Genesis 5:25-29)

Methuselah

I was the one sent from the ark
To see when we could disembark.
  I showed that there'd soon be relief
  By bringing back an olive leaf.

    Who am I?

(Genesis 8:11)
əʌop

Knock, knock.
Who's there?
Noah.
Noah who?
Noah lot of reasons to trust the Lord!

All houses have a front door;
  most have a back door, too.
But just how many doors were put
  in Noah's floating zoo?

(Genesis 6:16)

əuo

Noah's offspring numbered three.
  (Good children every one!)
You can show how smart you are
  if you can name each son.

(Genesis 6:10)

Shem, Ham, Japheth

Noah built the ark with skill,
   bottom, top, and sides.
You may know how long and tall,
   but do you know how wide?

(Genesis 6:15)

75 feet

The ark was so impressive
   as it stretched up to the sky.
It loomed above the dry ground.
   Can you tell me just how high?

(Genesis 6:15)

45 feet

The ark had to be painted,
   each crevice, nook, and crack.
The substance was so sticky;
   the color was so black.

What did Noah use to keep the ark from
   leaking?

(Genesis 6:14)

pitch

It's important to remember
relatives from long ago.
Tell me Noah's great-grandfather
if his name you think you know.

(Genesis 5:21)

Enoch

Noah's father was a good man.
(But his name was rather odd!)
He loved his son most dearly
and taught him to serve God.

Who was Noah's father?

(Genesis 5:28-29)

Lamech

Water poured down from the sky—
all day and then all night.
Do you know how long it rained
without the sun in sight?

(Genesis 7:4)

40 days and 40 nights

When the flood was over
the waters drained away.
The process was a slow one.
It took how many days?

(Genesis 8:3)

150 days

Noah sent out two birds
from the rain-soaked ark.
The first had blackish feathers
and eyes both keen and dark.

Name this bird.

(Genesis 8:7)

raven

A bird was sent by Noah
to scan both north and south.
It came back in the evening.
What was in its mouth?

(Genesis 8:11)

olive branch

The ark at last completed
its long and soggy quest.
Can you name the mountain where
it finally came to rest?

(Genesis 8:4)

Mt. Ararat

When Noah left the ark and knelt
on dry land once again,
what was the first thing that he built
while watched by all his kin?

(Genesis 8:20)

altar to God

God made a vow to Noah:
All life would never die.
He sealed it with a symbol
placed high up in the sky.

What did God put up in the sky?

(Genesis 9:13)

a rainbow

I spoke out against King Herod
  Who had taken his brother's wife.
I lost my head for the cause of God
  But gained eternal life.

Who am I?

(Matthew 14:1-12)

John the Baptist

I wanted to be a man of God,
  A man who sent Satan reeling.
But when I tried to walk to the Lord
  I got this sinking feeling.

Who am I?

(Matthew 14:22-33)

Peter

When the animals entered the ark
  Noah feared he'd forgotten the fleas.
Until he found two taking a nap
  Inside of the shaggy sheep's fleece.

No one in Moab could grow any grain.
  It finally became quite gruesome.
So Ruth and Naomi set out on foot
  For Bethlehem, where people grew some!

Question: How could Noah see out the window of the ark?

Answer: He used his windshield vipers!

The Israelites were a cranky bunch
who wanted more than bread for lunch.
They moaned and groaned and stomped
their feet.
God showed them how to make ends
meat.

What kind of meat did God send them to
eat?

(Exodus 16:9-13)

quail

Good Enoch did all evil shun.
His faith in God was one-on-one.
And when his life on earth was done
He rose to the occasion!

(Genesis 5:24)

Christ's hunger brought him pangs of grief.
The fig tree offered no relief.
"Cursed be this tree
That denies fruit to me!"
It never again would re-leaf.

(Matthew 21:18-22)

The plagues were toadily awesome!
  They were as lice as lice could be.
It boiled down to the frightening
  As God worked his plan out gnaturally.

It was an expensive lesson.
  No lo-cust truth was that.
The Egyptians learned the dark way
  God's will you can't combat!

Through me God did something grand
When he led his people
  to the Promised Land.
My name rhymes with "roses."
Yes, that's right! I am _____.

Moses

There once was a mean king named Pharaoh
Who wanted God's people for slaves, so
  God sent Moses and Aaron
  And when they were all done
The king cried, "Oh, please! Won't you *all go!*"

(Exodus 12:31-32)

Aaron used it to work wonders
  Before the Pharaoh's court.
When magicians tried to do the same,
  Theirs all came up short.

What was it?

(Exodus 7:8-12)

staff

Question: What was Moses' favorite dessert?
Answer: *Manna-creme* pie!

Moses was never good at math.
   (Fractions he couldn't abide!)
But when he came to the roaring Red Sea
   He was glad he could divide!

DRY, DRY AGAIN

The scene was set for a great, big fight.
The Egyptian army was in sight.
But Israel shook and moaned until
the Lord commanded them, "Be still!"

Then he told Moses, "Lift your staff
and split this mighty sea in half.
Let Pharaoh and his army see
that all your battles are fought by *me!*"

So with a wave of Moses' hand
the people crossed on bone-dry land.
And when they reached the other side
the water crashed in a churning tide.

It buried that army,
    horse and hoof.
And to the Lord's power
    gave absolute proof!

(Exodus 14:5-29)

I used a rock to pillow my head.
On the cold, hard earth I made my bed.
A ladder to heaven I dreamed,
With angels a-flutter, a-gleam.

Who am I?

(Genesis 28:10-12)
Jacob

I gave away my birthright
For a bowl of lentil soup.
How often I regretted being
Such a nincompoop!

Who am I?

(Genesis 25:24-34)
Esau

I should have looked beneath the veil
My bride wore on that day.
For my lovely Rachel's sister
Was the one I led away!

Who am I?

(Genesis 29:15-30)
Jacob

I was the one my dad adored.
He made a rainbow coat I wore.
But my brothers were jealous
And said, "Come, let's sell us
This dreamer who causes such fuss!"

Who am I?

(Genesis 37:3-4, 12-28)
Joseph

That king! He had a thing for fire—
he made the flames
higher and higher.
And then, with a grin,
he threw us three in.

But not even smoke
got on our attire.
And by God's great power—
we didn't perspire!

Who are we?

(Daniel 3:8-28)
Shadrach, Meshach, Abednego

To the shepherds I brought glad tidings
of the new Messiah's birth.
I sang, "Glory to God in the highest
and peace to men on earth."

Who am I?

(Luke 2:8-14)
angel

I was the humble cradle
where Mary's baby lay.
I kept him safe and cozy
on a bed of fragrant hay.

What am I?

(Luke 2:4-7)
manger

Mary and Joseph brought to the temple
their special, newborn son.
I was the priest who held him and knew
he was God's Anointed One.

Who am I?

(Luke 2:25-32)
Simeon

49

I was related to Jesus.
(Our mothers were cousins, you see.)
I lived in the desert and dressed rather crude.
"Repent!" was my loud, constant plea.

Who am I?

(Matthew 3:1-4)
John the Baptist

I'm not what you'd call famous—
Though I was a disciple of Christ.
When I asked my brother to meet the Lord
He listened to my advice.

Who am I?

(John 1:40-41)
Andrew

My given name was Simon,
But when Jesus saw me he said:
"No longer Simon, you shall be
Called 'the Rock' instead."

Who am I?

(John 1:42)
Peter

We were a family of fishermen.
My sons were James and John.
We were mending nets when Christ called to
    them,
    "Come! Follow!"—and then they were
    gone.

Who am I?

(Mark 1:19-20)
Zebedee

My waves raged high against their boat.
    Their hearts with fear I did instill.
Till Jesus woke and tamed me with
    His quiet words of, "Peace, be still!"

What am I?

(Matthew 8:23-26)
Sea of Galilee

51

WHO ARE WE?

'Twas a lumpy situation!
  The new king we could not find.
And for nights on end we'd traveled
  On a trail of strange star-shine.

He was not in Herod's palace.
  (Where we thought that he would be!)
And our chances now to find him
  Seemed as weak as camel fleas.

But the scribes soon found the answer,
  For the prophets had foretold:
"Now in Bethlehem of Judea
  Shall be born a ruler bold."

So there we sought and found him,
  Offered to him gifts so rare.
At his majesty and beauty
  We could only, speechless, stare.

Then we climbed aboard our camels
  For the bumpy, long trip back—
Praising God and feeling happy,
  Getting eager to unpack!

(Matthew 2:1-12)
the Three Wise Men

52

A stone to make men stumble;
A rock to make them fall.
Yet this redeeming figure
Is Savior to us all.

Name him.

To meet the heathen, well-armed foe
A braver man could not be found.
He led the battle of Jericho
And its walls came tumbling down.

Name this leader.

I tied foxes together
And set them on fire.
My incredible strength
All men did admire.

Who am I?

I heard my name called in the night;
  I thought it was rather odd.
When Eli the priest summoned me,
  the speaker was really God.

  Who am I?

(I Samuel 3:1-11)
Samuel

You know me as the one God sent
So Nineveh could all repent.
To visit those heathens was not my wish.
I took a detour inside a great fish.

    Who am I?

(Jonah, chs. 1–4)
Jonah

God told me to get up and go
Unto a place I did not know.
If to this plan I would agree
All people would be blessed through me.

    Who am I?

(Genesis 12:1-3)
Abraham

My mother-in-law Naomi
Was my closest friend.
And after the death of both her sons
On me she did depend.

I returned with her to Bethlehem
As the barley harvest began.
I went out in search of grain for us—
But found myself a man!

Who am I?

(Ruth, chs. 1–4)

Ruth

The fleece was dry;
the fleece was wet,
So that I never
would forget
The power of God when
I started to fret.

Who am I?

(Judges 6:36-40)

Gideon

57

DON'T YOU HATE IT WHEN . . .

Don't you hate it when it's your turn to clean out the stalls—and the elephants have diarrhea?

Noah

Don't you hate it when you have to eat leftovers?

Adam

Don't you hate it when the king invites you to lunch—and you *are* lunch?

Daniel

Don't you hate it when you get nagged about forgetting your anniversary—by all seven hundred of your wives?

Solomon

Don't you hate it when you have sand in your shoes—for forty years!

Moses

Don't you hate it when just *anybody* cuts your hair?

Don't you hate it when the "catch of the day" is *you?*

Don't you hate it when first thing in the morning you have to fight a giant—and you only have five rocks?

61

Don't you hate it when everybody on the beach is hungry—and you're the only one who brought a sack lunch?

Boy with loaves and fishes

Don't you hate it when you stand in water all day and your toes end up looking like bleached prunes?

John the Baptist

Don't you hate it when you have to eat like a bird?

Elijah

Don't you hate it when you have only one headlight?

Wise man

Don't you hate it when life is the pits?

Joseph (son of Jacob)

Don't you hate it when the whole place is
constantly jumpin'?

Pharaoh

Don't you hate it when you have to watch your baby brother and he's all wet?

Miriam

Don't you hate it when everybody at the pool wants to be the first one in?

Man at Pool of Bethesda

Don't you hate it when Jesus walks on water and you can't even swim?

Peter

His days were dark as starless night
For Bartimaeus had no sight.
  Till Jesus came by
  And touched his blind eyes,
Giving him life and true Light.

(Mark 10:46-52)

I was a wee bit rattled
  When the Lord said I should preach
To a valley full of old dry bones
  That desert sun had bleached.

But as I spoke the word of God
  The bones joined—joint to joint.
And became a mighty army
  That the Lord could then anoint.

  Who am I?

(Ezekiel 37:1-10)

Ezekiel

ELIJAH'S EULOGY

The finest moment of my life
  Came at its final hour.
God sent a special taxi-cab
  Loaded with horse power!

(II Kings 2:9-12 will tell you about God's powerful
"taxi-cab" and Elijah's grand exit.)

There once was a virgin named Mary
Whose life was oh so ordinary.
  Till Gabriel appeared
  And said, "Do not fear!
The promised Messiah you carry!"

(Luke 1:26-35)

Shepherds on Judean hills
Hadn't hoped for such a thrill.
  What radiant light!
  And angels in white!
The prophecy at last fulfilled!

(Luke 2:8-20)

67

GIDEON

He was just a simple farmer
  Who in secret threshed his wheat.
For the Midianites who roamed the land
  Hadn't left him much to eat.

But Jehovah sent a message,
  (By an angel it was taken)
Saying, "Greetings, mighty warrior!
  By the Lord you're not forsaken."

So he cast aside his farm tools,
  Took up a sword instead,
Fought those hordes of evil
  Till in safety he broke bread.

(Judges 6:11-12; 7:1-22)

DIP, DIP, DIP . . .

The mighty soldier Naaman
   came to seek Elisha's aid.
To be freed from his dread sickness
   a king's ransom he'd have paid!

But the prophet sent his servant
   with this message to deliver:
"Lay aside your fancy clothing
   and go dip in Jordan's river."

Now Naaman was insulted
   when Elisha did suggest
washing in that muddy water
   would his leprosy arrest.

But at his servant's urging
   he did as the prophet said—
and his skin became as healthy
   as a baby's smooth forehead!

(II Kings 5:1-14)

HOT SPOT

Elijah challenged
  the prophets of Baal
To call down fire
  from their idol so frail.

But try as they might
No spark was in sight.

With a whoosh of fire
God did prevail!

(I Kings 18:20-39)

He was going to the temple
  When he saw the crippled man.
Peter said, "I have no money—
  But I'll give you what I can."

What did Peter give the man?

(Acts 3:1-8)

healing

Of their real estate transaction
They decided just a fraction
　　To the church they'd give,
　　But neither one lived
To savor ill-got satisfaction.

Who were this greedy couple?

(Acts 5:1-10)
Ananias and Sapphira

SEW-SO

I was a simple seamstress
  Making clothes for Joppa's poor.
Then a sudden sickness laid me low
  And everyone was sure
My days on earth were over—
  Death hasn't any cure!

But Peter heard and quickly came.
  He turned the others out.
He prayed and then he touched my hand.
  "Get up!" I heard him shout.
And so I did! This wonder told
  Turned many souls from doubt.

Who am I?

(Acts 9:36-42)
Dorcas (or Tabitha)

RHODA

Of course she heard the knocking.
(It was too loud to ignore!)
Then she recognized the voice
That gently did implore,
"I'm free! I'm free! Now let me in
And I shall tell you more."
With joy she ran to tell the news—
    but forgot
    to unlock
    the door!

Whom did Rhoda leave standing outside
    the door?

Acts 12:6-17
Peter

78

DISCIPLES' DILEMMA
Matthew 14:13-21

Five thousand persons stayed for lunch
And none of us had half a hunch
What all these hungry mouths would
munch.

But Jesus seemed quite calm and said,
"We have some fish, a little bread."
He blessed it and those people fed.

A miracle! Imagine this:
Five thousand fed from two small fishes!
Leftover scraps that filled twelve dishes!

OF KINGS AND QUEENS

Knock, knock.
Who's there?
Saul.
Saul who?
Saul that matters is to love the Lord!

Knock, knock.
Who's there?
Ahab.
Ahab who?
A-hab the Bible to show me what's right!

I won a beauty contest
And became a Persian queen.
But because of wicked Haman
I soon found myself between
His cruel plot and my own people.
God helped me intervene
And sent his righteous judgment on
Those enemies so mean.

Who am I?

(Esther, chs. 1–10)
Esther

One hundred Philistines took a fall so I could
become Saul's son-in-law.

Who am I?

(I Samuel 18:24-27)
David

This king sent down a sword and shield
For David on the battlefield.
But David said, "I'd rather not.
I'll trust in God and my slingshot."

Who was king of Israel when David
killed Goliath?

(I Samuel 17:38-40)
Saul

In Israel there lived a king
Who understood most *everything*.
From civil disputes to cultural pursuits,
His wisdom was absolute.

Who was Israel's wisest king?

(I Kings 4:29-34)
Solomon

Jesse fathered eight strong sons
And loved them each and every one.
But of them all, the youngest proved
The one on whom God's spirit moved.

So Samuel did the holy thing:
Anointed him as Israel's king.

Name Jesse's youngest son.

(I Samuel 16:1-13)

David

There once was a great queen named Esther
Who had to become a protester.
   Her people she saved
   By an act that was brave.
God honored her prayers and he blessed her.

DAVID'S DITTY

A shepherd's job is pretty tough.
He works in mountains wild and rough
Where beasts sneak down on padded
feet
And try his lambs and ewes to eat.

His best friends are
His harp and sling.
He learns to fight;
He learns to sing.

He spends his nights
In grateful prayer,
Knowing God is
everywhere!

I held a beauty pageant
  To pick myself a queen.
The contestants were all lovely;
  Competition was quite keen
Until fair Esther showed her face.
  Such beauty I'd never seen!

     Who am I?

(Esther 2:1-17)
King Xerxes (or Ahasuerus)

COMPANY COMIN'

In my far-away country
I heard of his fame.
Such wealth and such wisdom
None other could claim.

So I made the long journey
And brought gifts of worth
To give to this monarch—
The wisest on earth!

Who am I?

(I Kings 10:1-10)
Queen of Sheba

EXECUTIVE DECISION

King Agrippa came for a visit.
(Bernice came with him, too.)
They were met by Festus,
who wrung his hands
And said, "I'm in a stew!"

It seems he had a prisoner, Paul,
And the Jews all wanted him dead.
But Festus found no evil
In what he did or said.

So they brought him before King Agrippa
(Himself quite a scholar on law).
And Paul preached a powerful sermon
To all who were in the hall.

"Come, be a Christian!" Paul urged
As Agrippa stroked his beard.
"Not now," the king said, rising to go—
More anxious than he appeared.

For the truth of Paul's message
had struck him
More deeply than any would know.
And he kept his pride, but lost his soul
With the force of that final "No!"

(Acts 25:13–26:31)

When those crafty wise men tricked me
  I felt like a royal fool.
So I ordered all babies murdered.
  I almost enjoy being cruel!

  Who am I?

(Matthew 2:16)
Herod

I was married to King Ahab.
(We were a wicked twosome!)
I taught idol worship to Israel—
And heathen practices gruesome.

  Who am I?

(I Kings 16:30-33)
Jezebel

ROWDY RIDDLES

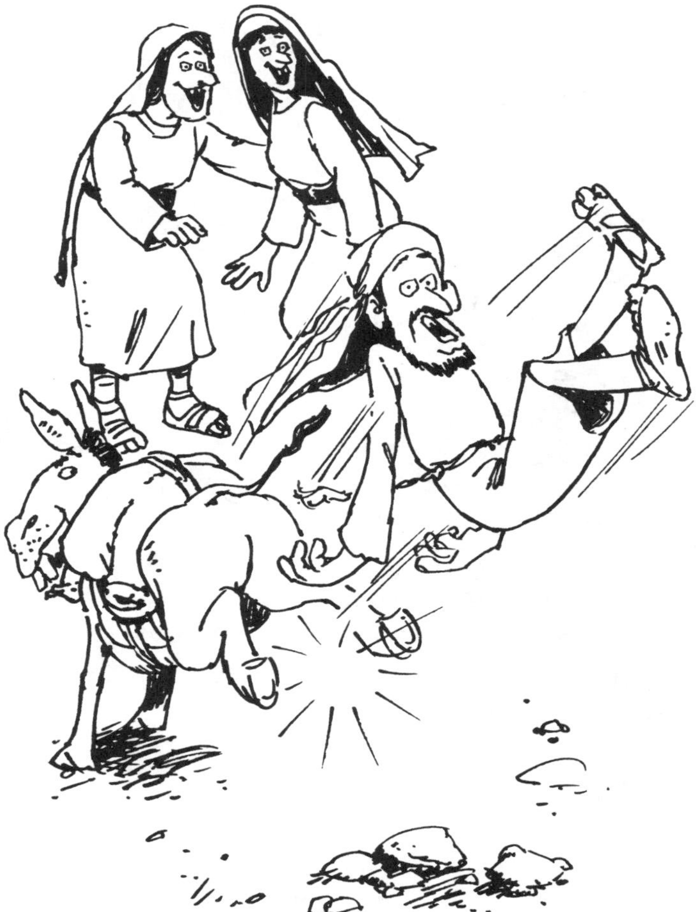

These cities were so wicked,
  They made the good Lord mad.
He hurled fire down upon their heads
  Because they were so bad.

Name these two cities.

(Genesis 18:20; 19:24-25)
Sodom and Gomorrah

God sent plagues on Egypt.
In all they numbered ten.
Can you name the second one?
It was totally, toadily grim!

(Exodus 8:1-15)

frogs

Question: Why was Elijah able to outrun Ahab's chariot?

(Read all about it in I Kings 18:44-46.)

Answer: Because Elijah was powered by the Lord, and Ahab's chariot was just two-tired!

I was a beast of burden
  But God made me wise
And showed me the danger
  Unseen by some eyes.
When I talked to my master,
  He sure was surprised!

     What am I?

                    (Numbers 22:21-31)
                         donkey

Every morning and each evening
  Goliath made his way
Down to challenge Israel's army.
  This went on for days and days!

How many days?

(I Samuel 17:16)
forty

Jesse was a loving father,
  And carefully he chose
Bread to send his sons the soldiers.
  Do you know how many loaves?

(I Samuel 17:17)
ten

David met Goliath
  With a slingshot and a stick.
Do you know the number of
  Stones he stopped to pick?

(I Samuel 17:40)
five

100

Bigger than a butterfly,
    Smaller than a yak.
Jesus rode into Jerusalem
    Sitting on my back.

What am I?

(Matthew 21:1-11)
donkey (or colt)

Jesus went into the desert
    Where he fasted and he prayed
To prepare for his great mission.
    He was there how many days?

(Matthew 4:1-2)
40 days

THERE'S NO PLACE LIKE HOME, REALLY!

Jesus tells the story
  of a boy who thought he knew
Exactly where he'd like to go
  and what he'd like to do.

He said, "I'll go see father;
  his servant I'll become.
After all the things I've done
  I can't be called a son."

When finally he saw his home
tears flowed from his eyes.
His father met him in the road
and gave him a surprise.

What did the father do when his lost son
returned home?

I am only a poor widow—
my offering is pitifully small.
Yet God has accepted this simple gift
because I am giving my all.

What did the widow put into the temple
offering?

(Luke 21:1-4)

two very small copper coins

I was a tax collector
Till Jesus came my way.
Then I became a disciple
And wrote a book still read today.

Who am I?

(Matthew 9:9)

Matthew

Jesus tells the story
of a lamb that lost its way.
The shepherd left his other sheep
to seek this frightened stray.

How many sheep did the shepherd leave
behind to go searching for that one
lost lamb?

(Matthew 18:12-13)

ninety-nine

PARABLE OF THE SOWER
(Matthew 13:3-8)

I am the seed that fell on the path
  where all could see.
What happened to me?

birds ate

I am the seed that fell on rocky soil.
Such a calamity!
What happened to me?

sun scorched

I am the seed that fell among thorns.
My end was agony!
What happened to me?

choked by weeds

I am the seed that fell on good ground
And plunged my roots down joyfully.
What happened to me?

grew and produced a crop

The poor man was beaten by robbers
And left on the road to die.
A priest and a Levite saw his distress
But hurriedly passed on by.

A stranger from Samaria
Also happened that way.
Seeing the wounded man suffer
Filled him with dismay.

What did the Samaritan do?

(Luke 10:33-34)

He bandaged the man's wounds and took him to an inn and cared for him.

There once were some men who felt able
To build a great tower whose gable
    Would reach to the sky.
    It was only so high
Before God caused the whole crew to Babel.

(Did you ever wonder why there are so many languages in the world? You can read about it in Genesis 11:1-9.)

There once was a fortified city
Who worshiped false gods—what a pity!
  Joshua marched 'round its walls
  Till they crashed—what a fall!
The air with its rubble was gritty.

(You can read about this city, Jericho, in the Old Testament book of Joshua, chapter 6.)

There once was a man named Zacchaeus
Who wanted the Savior to see as
  He passed by that day.
  He heard Jesus say,
"We'll share some dinner as soon as
    You come down from that branch
    And give me a chance
  To show you that I am the Way."

(Luke 19:1-10)

Abram's story needs to be told.
His vision was big; his face bold.
　　God promised a son.
　　And, sure 'nough, it was done—
When he was a hundred years old.

(Genesis 21:5)